Hear then, the Parable

Rev. Shea Zellweger

Copyright © 2012 Shea Zellweger

All rights reserved.

ISBN: **1480192961**
ISBN-13: **978-1480192966**

DEDICATION

For Jocie, my perpetual supporter.

Contents

Introduction iii

1 Hermas' Location 1

2 The Oral Nature of the *Shepherd* 16

3 The *Shepherd* as Homily 26

4 the Homiletical Model(s) of the *Shepherd* 42

Appendix 51

Bibliography 54

ACKNOWLEDGMENTS

Thanks goes out to the many who have made this text possible particularly the following:
Bill Herzog, my advisor, who believed in this project and encouraged me to chase it.
Carolyn Osiek, the foremost authority on the *Shepherd*, who was willing to answer my questions and help me to find resources without expecting anything in return.
Mike Fraley and Aaron Zellweger, who served as faithful sounding boards for ideas which did not really matter to them.

Introduction

The development of the Christian homily has been a topic of interest for scholars for many years. As Stewart-Sykes (2001) has demonstrated, the distinction between prophecy and homily in the early Church was muddled, if indeed it existed at all. He notes that Justin is "the first indisputable witness to a homily relating to a preceding scriptural reading," (2001, 6) which makes the first half of the second century the latest point for such a homily to have developed. Among other early Christian authors, Stewart-Sykes offers Hermas, author of *The Shepherd* as providing an example of a pre-Justinian homily (2001, 109). While Stewart-Sykes focuses on the 7th Mandate of *The Shepherd* of Hermas as clear scripture-based homily, this study examines the broader work of Hermas in an effort to demonstrate the homiletical nature of the text, and to propose a distinct homiletical model based on the methodology employed by Hermas- a methodology of exposition through narrative and metaphor, rather than rhetorical or analytical evaluation.

Overview of Chapters
Chapter 1- Hermas's Location
This chapter investigates the text and authorship of the *Shepherd*. How many authors there were, who they were, and when they might

have written are all examined. This is followed by a discussion of how best to classify the genre of the *Shepherd*.

Chapter 2- The Oral Nature of the *Shepherd*
The discussion of generic classification of the *Shepherd* is continued in this chapter, in which it is argued that standard classifications for textual genre are not truly applicable to the text, because it is primarily oral literature. The works of Carolyn Osiek and Walter Ong are examined in an effort to demonstrate the oral nature of the text.

Chapter 3- The *Shepherd* as Homily
Chapter 3 deals first with the difficulty of identifying homiletic material in a culture which relies heavily on oral dissemination of information. A broader definition of homily which accounts for this difficulty is proposed. The remainder of the chapter investigates several portions of the *Shepherd* in an effort to identify their dependence upon tradition, in order to establish the text has homily, rather than truly original content. Potential relationships between the *Shepherd* and traditions preserved in the Christian Bible are identified, discussed, and evaluated for their likelihood of relationship.

Chapter 4- The Homiletical Model(s) of the *Shepherd*
Those portions of the *Shepherd* which are determined to have a strong likelihood of relationship to extant texts are examined in order to determine the manner in which Hermas went about utilizing traditions to produce his homilies. An attempt is then made to reconstruct the model which Hermas used for writing homilies. Finally, an argument is made for the utilization of this model in contemporary contexts.

Appendix- In the Garden of Joy ch. 2
This appendix is the author's original content, written in an effort to use the recreated method of Hermas in a contemporary context. It is a brief example, intended for a small group Bible study rather than a homily written for delivery to a congregation.

1 Hermas' Location

The *Shepherd* of Hermas has interested and puzzled Christian audiences for as long as the New Testament itself (possibly longer than some books). While the book has been popular since its early days, there have been multiple questions about the nature of the text, and most of them have existed since the 2nd Century. Under dispute historically were the authorship, authenticity, orthodoxy, canonicity, and value of the *Shepherd*, with prominent voices offering extremely disparate positions on each of these matters. In more recent discussions, the former questions remain disputed, but have been joined by new speculation over the genre, number of authors, and location of the original writing. While there have been multiple times when a scholarly consensus was formed on each of these matters, that agreement has invariably been challenged at some later time, and consensus has repeatedly given way to dispute. While the ultimate goal of this thesis is to present a new perspective on the nature of the text of the *Shepherd*, it is necessary to first review the existing disagreements, and demonstrate my own position on those disputed matters which pertain directly to the ultimate question of homily to which this paper is devoted.

The Authorship of the *Shepherd*.

The details surrounding the authorship of the Shepherd have been disputed since Antiquity. Origen contended that the text had been written in the middle of the first century by the Hermas mentioned in Romans 16[1] while the author of the Muratorian Canon claimed the author was the brother of Pope Pius I in the middle of the second century.[2] With the onset of higher criticism, further questions were raised. Several who studied Hermas asserted multiple authorship of the text, with as many as six distinct authors or redactors being postulated.[3]

As Carolyn Osiek states in the opening sentence of her commentary on the *Shepherd*, "No other noncanonical writing was as popular before the fourth century as the *Shepherd of Hermas*."[4] Thankfully, this popularity led to an abundance of manuscripts, such that today "It is the most frequently attested postcanonical text in the surviving Christian manuscripts of Egypt well into the fifth century."[5]

The author makes multiple autobiographical statements throughout the course of the text. While Dibelius is inclined to read the text figuratively and believes that these claims should not be trusted as historically accurate,[6] Osiek suggests that the autobiographical information can most likely be trusted, arguing that a
"more nuanced interpretation would be that there is a basis of historicity upon which the author builds to emphasize his message. Thus the text contains a mixture of biography and literary reworking, so that the family becomes a literary mirror of the whole community."[7]

---

[1] Ehrman, Bart D. 2003. *The Apostolic Fathers*. Edited by J. Henderson. Vol. 25, *The Loeb Classical Library*. Cambridge, MA: Harvard College. 167

[2] Ehrman, Bart D. 2003A. *Lost Scriptures: Books That Did Not Make It into the New Testament*. New York: Oxford University Press. 332

[3] Osiek, Carolyn. 1999. *Shepherd of Hermas: A Commentary on the Shepherd of Hermas*. Edited by H. Koester, *Hermeneia*. Minneapolis: Augsburg Fortress Press. 9

[4] Ibid, 1

[5] Ibid, 2

[6] Dibelius, Dr. Martin. 1923. Zweites Gleichnis. In *Der Hirt des Hermas*. Tubingen: Verlag Von J. C. B. Mohr. 419-20, 449

[7] *Commentary* 24

If Hermas was in fact known to his community (an idea which will be further investigated later), it stands to reason that the autobiographical information would be accurate, as it could be verified by his audience. But since the life of Hermas is not the primary focus of this text, it is most likely that the information he chooses to include about himself is selected and framed in such a way as to enforce the message he is attempting to convey, hence the "literary reworking;" Hermas has an agenda in mind, and any autobiographical information, however accurate, is shared because it furthers that agenda.

The Shepherd begins with a short autobiographical statement: "Ὁ θρεψας με πέπρακέν με 'Ροδῃ τινὶ εἰς 'Ρώμην' μετὰ πολλὰ ἔτη ταύτην ἀνεγρωρισαμην καὶ ἠρξάμην αὐτὴν ἀγαπαν ὡς ἀδελφήν." (Vis. I.1). Osiek notes the significance of Hermas describing "himself as a *threptos*, a term most often used to refer to a foundling, an abandoned child brought up as a slave in another household. In the Roman world, this was the most common form of family-size control." She later points out that "the manumission of a young adult slave was not unusual in urban areas" We learn from this introduction that Hermas is a freedman, most likely from an urban area- which most scholars agree is Rome.[8] Later in the text, the audience learns from one of his visions that Hermas was formerly rich. "Ἀπο σεαυτου πρωτον γνωθυ ὅτε ἐπλούτεις ἄχρηστος ἦς, νυν δὲ εὔχρηστος εἶ καὶ ὠφέλιμος τῃ ζωῃ."[9] However, the rest of the text makes it clear that while he may no longer be rich, Hermas is far from destitute. He owns a house[10] and may also possess farmland; Vis. III.1.2 refers to "τὸν αγρὸν ὅπου χονδρίζεις" but the text is never explicit as to whether Hermas owns the land he farms, or if he is a tenant farmer. A later passage which does not mention Hermas by name is probably a close approximation of his own situation; Similitude IX.30.5 also talks about those whose riches have been cut away, and asserts that they

---

[8] Ibid 18

[9] *Vision* III.6.7

[10] *Vision* V.1

are not removed entirely, so that the formerly rich might be able to do something good with what they have left over.

With each of these autobiographical passages in mind, a picture of the historical Hermas comes into focus. A freedman who had received some degree of training and education from his mistress, Hermas saw success in business and agriculture. At some point, either due to his conversion to Christianity, or a later attempt to demonstrate a deeper commitment, Hermas committed a significant portion of his belongings to God, most likely by way of his local church. In a movement which was primarily popular among the impoverished and disenfranchised, the presence of someone who could finance the operations of the church would have been significant in its own right, and while Hermas may not have been the spiritual authority in his house church, his financial contribution would have made him a prominent member of the community. It is unlikely that a single church had multiple such sponsors, so Hermas' position in the congregation would have been unique as well. If we can accept this depiction of Hermas, then it is reasonable to conclude that Hermas was very likely the *paterfamilias* of his house church. However, there are several issues which must be addressed in order to embrace such a position.

A major challenge to this perspective on Hermas' portrayal of himself is found in the debate over the number of authors who had a hand in writing the *Shepherd*, which is based primarily upon the apparent differences between sections of the text. The *Shepherd* is comprised of three distinct sections, known as the *Visions*, the *Mandates* (or *Commandments*), and the *Similitudes* (or *Parables*). The *Visions* are generally agreed upon as the oldest portion of the text, and contained within them are multiple references to Hermas by name. Apart from Hermas, the most significant character is an old woman, representing the Church, who is the mediator of Hermas' revelations. In contrast, Hermas is not addressed by name after *Vision* V, and the woman is replaced as mediator by a shepherd (from whom the text receives its name). There are additional linguistic variances between the *Visions* and the remainder of the text, most notably the references to Hermas' αδελφοι which are regular in the *Visions* and not present throughout the *Mandates* and *Similitudes*. These differences were sufficient for some contemporary scholars to see separation in authorship between the major sections of the text, but it is likely that many had ulterior motives for doing so. As Osiek notes, there is ancient reference to at least two, and possibly three, distinct authors:[11] The text had been attributed by Origen to the Hermas of *Romans* 16:14 (c. 60), and by the *Muratorian Canon* to the brother of Pius I (c. 140). Additionally, there is an internal reference by the author to Clement, apparently a contemporary, who is generally assumed to be Clement of Rome (c. 100). It is highly unlikely that these were all the same person, and literary critics appeared hesitant to conclude that members of the original audience such as Origen were wrong, so they saw in the text the differences necessary for all early witnesses to be correct.

These literary demarcations proved insufficient to support claims of separate authorship in their own right, and the field eventually returned to agreement that the most likely scenario was single authorship, although this agreement was hedged on the possibility of multiple sources and a single redactor. Recently, however, Roger Bagnall has re-opened the discussion on the basis of papyrology. Instead of a single autograph or redaction, he states that

"It is, rather, a combination of two originally autonomous collections. One of these is made up of the four books of the *Visions*, and the other of the *Precepts* and *Similitudes*, with the addition, by way of preface, of what is generally numbered as the fifth book of the *Visions*. Carlini provides a list of the papyrus codices that one can show, or at least argue with some probability, to have contained only one of these two original works."[12]

While this gives some weight to the literary distinctions made by former scholars, and will no doubt be used in the future to promote a return to theories of multiple authorship, it does not truly add any barriers to the single authorship proposal which were not already present. The division of the text among *Visions* I-IV, *Vision* V, and the *Mandates* and *Similitudes* has been proposed in the past, as detailed above. That the *Visions* might be an earlier work is likewise something which has previously been theorized. Bagnall's

---

[11] Osiek. *Commentary*, 8-9

[12] Bagnall, Roger S. 2009. *Early Christian Books in Egypt*. Princeton: Princeton University Press. 45

work simply adds textual evidence to support a former conclusion. Scholars now must accept that two sections of the text were disseminated independently of one another very early in the text's existence (although the papyri mentioned are all dated to several decades after the initial authorship). Proponents of single authorship, however, need only conclude that the same author wrote two texts, distributed them separately, and eventually combined them into a single text with an additional passage to bridge the two works together. Since Bagnall's work does not provide literary evidence of separate authorship, but rather papyrological evidence of separate distribution, it should not be seen as significant in theories of authorship.

Dating the *Shepherd* is equally as difficult as determining the number of authors. As stated above, there are at least three potential time frames for the writing of the *Shepherd*- the mid-first century, the turn of the second century, and the mid-second century. Support for the earliest date comes from Origen, who asserts that the author is the same Hermas who is saluted by Paul in Romans 16. If this is the case, the text could have been written any time in the few decades following the crucifixion of Jesus.[13] However, Origen clearly views the *Shepherd* as Scripture, and as such, it is likely that his bias would have been to date it as early as possible, in order to justify its inclusion in his canon.

The latest date is offered by the *Muratorian Canon*, which identifies the author of the *Shepherd* as the brother of Pius I, and the text was written while Pius held the bishopric of Rome. If this is accurate, the text was written between 140 and 161, depending on when Pius' reign is dated. However, the validity and dating of the canon in question has come under scrutiny in recent decades. While many see it has having been written by a contemporary of Pius (and therefore Hermas) Albert C. Sundberg, Jr. puts forth a

---

[13] While most have concluded that Hermas' writing would have followed Paul's letter to the Romans, this is not necessitated by Origen's claim. If the author was, in fact, known to Paul, there is no reason to assume he was not in the practice of writing prior to Paul's salutation.

compelling case for dating the *Muratorian Canon* in the 4th century,[14] which would remove it some 200 years from the time of Pius. By that time, the *Shepherd* had already begun to fall out of favor with the church as a whole (except possibly in Alexandria), so the prevailing bias would have favored a later date, in order to have as much separation between the time of the Apostles and the writing of the *Shepherd*. Additionally, Eusebius wrote about Hermas, brother of Pius I, without making any reference to him as the potential author of the *Shepherd*.[15]

The final potential date, approximately half way between the early and late proposals, relies on the internal testimony of the *Shepherd*. *Vision* II.4.3 contains instructions for someone named Clement to distribute copies of the *Shepherd* abroad, stating that doing so is his job. There are known possibilities for both the earliest and latest proposals for dating, with varying degrees of likelihood. Clement of Alexandria was born c. 150, so there is a very slim chance that he could have been old enough to serve as a scribe to the church by the time Hermas was prepared to distribute his work, but this is highly unlikely, and no scholar supports this association. In support of the other extreme, Paul mentions someone named Clement as a fellow worker in *Philippians* 4:3. *Philippians* is traditionally thought to have been written from Rome, so this Clement may have known the Hermas of *Romans* 16. Little more can be said about this connection than that it must be seen as a possibility. Both *Romans* and *Philippians* are generally considered to be genuinely Pauline texts, written within a few years of one another, making it entirely possible that Hermas and Clement could have known one another, and considered each other to be peers in the Church.

The final possibility for dating, opened exclusively by the reference to Clement, associates this reference with Clement I, who is thought to have been active in the late 1st century. There is a great

---

[14] Sundberg, Albert C, Jr. 1973. Canon Muratori: a Fourth Century List. *Harvard Theological Review* 66 (1):41.

[15] Eusebius. A. Church History. In *Nicene and Post-Nicene Fathers*, edited by P. Schaff. Grand Rapids: Christian Classics Ethereal Library. 4.11.6

deal of tradition associating Clement with the apostles, and some sources identify him with the aforementioned Clement in *Philippians* 4. There is ample reason to assume that this is the Clement intended by Hermas. We know that he wrote at least one international correspondence (*I Clement*), so Hermas would have reason to see this as a part of his office. While terms such as "bishop" or "pope" are most likely anachronisms when discussing a first century figure, it is possible that the prominence accorded to Clement was done so because he served as a representative of the churches in Rome, perhaps in corresponding with the churches of other geographic areas. Given this, identifying him as the Clement referenced by Hermas seems like the most likely conclusion. Acknowledging that both Hermas and Clement have been proposed as acquaintances of Paul's, and placing the date of *I Clement* at the turn of the 2nd century, we have a working date range for the *Shepherd* of c. 60 CE to c. 120 CE as the most probably time period for its writing.

With the above reasoning in mind, I propose that Hermas was a land owning member, and likely patron, of a late-First Century Christian house church. He held a significant degree of influence in his house church, great enough that he was permitted to instruct fellow believers in matters of faith. He had some personal knowledge of the author of *I Clement*, and appears to have believed that his own reputation would allow his writing to find an audience among Christians living in other regions who may not have known him personally.

The Audience of the *Shepherd*

We cannot know with certainty the makeup of Hermas' audience. He does not address the text to any person or group of people, and the only people named in the course of the text are Clement and Grapte, who are identified because of their roles in the broader church, rather than their standing in the local congregation. Still, there are several reasons to conclude that we can know something about the original intended audience. Maintaining Osiek's understanding of the family as "a literary mirror of the whole community,"[16] it is reasonable to assume that references to Hermas' wife and children are thinly veiled statements about the

---

[16] *Commentary* 24

congregation to which he belongs. These references are also concentrated in the earlier portions of the text, coinciding with the more frequent designation of the audience as "brothers"—a coincidence which seems to emphasize the deeper significance of Hermas' familial language.

The earliest familial reference takes place in the opening lines of the text, in which Hermas considers his former owner to be more attractive than his current wife. Shortly thereafter, his first heavenly guide appears to him in the form of an old (and presumably unattractive) woman, who, it is later revealed, is meant to represent the Church. This contrast of two women in the opening paragraphs, one representing his former life and the other his current life, sets the stage for an understanding of Hermas' "wife" as that to which he has committed his life. At the time he was writing, his commitment was to his local congregation, so it is safe to assume that references to Hermas' wife are meant to say something about that congregation. Similarly, as *Pater Familias* of his local congregation, it makes sense that Hermas would also be inclined to refer to them as his children. While this use of multiple metaphors to mean the same people might be confusing in the abstract, the text itself bears out the usage in such a way as to make it quite evident that this is what is occurring.

Familial references in the *Shepherd* are almost universally negative. As mentioned above, Hermas' wife is compared unfavorably to his former mistress. She is also said to be a gossip,[17] and is indirectly accused of adultery.[18] Hermas' children are made out to be undisciplined,[19] blasphemous,[20] wicked,[21] and divisive.[22] This collection of negative qualities offers an understanding of a congregation in shambles. They do not remain faithful to the

---

[17] *Vision* II.2.3

[18] *Mandate* I.1ff

[19] *Vision* 1.3.1

[20] *Vision* II.2.2

[21] *Vision* III.9.1

[22] *Vision* II.9.9

commandments given them, allow divisions to arise among them, and may even dabble in the practice of other religions.[23]

This information tells us that Hermas' audience is a group of people about whom he cares deeply, but that he may be growing tired of their failings. It also lets us know that the admonishments and reprimands are meant, first and foremost, for his congregation, although the inclusion of the command for Clement does indicate that he thinks they might have a broader application. Finally, the relationship of Hermas to his audience makes clear his reason for emphasizing the possibility of secondary repentance,[24] as he cares about these people and desires for them to reconcile themselves with God.

The Text of the *Shepherd*

Having introduced the author and his community, we now turn our attention to his work. As stated in brief above, the *Shepherd* of Hermas is comprised of three sections, includes heavenly mediators, and reveals some biographical information about the author. It was likely written in two parts, which were later joined into a longer work, but there is little reason to assume multiple authorship. The simple fact that two books were written does not imply that they had two authors, and other claims meant to support multiple authors are incomplete at best.

These claims are usually based on one of two things. First, there are linguistic oddities, such as the presence of the word αδελφοι in the first book, and its absence from the second. However, it could be noted that Paul uses χαρις and its derivatives six times in the relatively short text of *Philippians*, yet it is not found anywhere in the much longer text of *1 Corinthians*. These two epistles are universally accepted as Pauline despite this slight linguistic difference, so clearly such a distinction is not sufficient to warrant claims of multiple authorship. The second major claim involves both the change of angelic mediators, and the fact that the second mediator, the Shepherd, does not address Hermas by name.

---

[23] The metaphor of adultery is most frequently used in biblical literature to imply that people are consorting with other gods.

[24] This emphasis has been the focus of many studies of the *Shepherd*, but will not factor prominently in this paper.

That an author would introduce a new character, or that the new character would behave differently from other characters, is hardly sufficient grounds for claiming that there was a change in authorship which coincided with the introduction of the new character. So without any significant challenges to the claim, we will assume that Hermas wrote the entire text, albeit in two stages.

The three sections of the *Shepherd* are usually seen as taking on three distinct forms, and divided accordingly. The first section, called the *Visions*, is a series of events in which Hermas witnesses supernatural occurrences, and subsequently has them explained to him by an angelic mediator, the woman who represents the Church. Second come the *Mandates* (or *Commandments*), which is a collection of commands for Hermas and his community to follow, relayed by the second mediator (the Shepherd). Finally, the *Similitudes* (or *Parables*) are stories told and subsequently explained by the *Shepherd*. While these general categories are useful for dividing the book, and for quick reference, they are not entirely accurate. *Vision* II, for instance, is only a vision insofar as Hermas sees his mediator, which is true for all three sections of the text. On the other hand *Similitude* IX, the longest of the parables, is actually a vision in which the Shepherd shows Hermas a series of events and explains them to him. The *Mandates* also rely heavily on figurative imagery, making them parabolic in nature, and are relayed by an angelic mediator, making them just as much visions as *Vision* II. So, while the classification system is useful in identifying specific passages (indeed, I use its conventions throughout this paper), it is not entirely helpful in delineating the makeup of a given portion of the text. In that regard, it would be best to view the entire book as a collection of visions, each containing parabolic elements, and each offering a command or set of commands.

While each individual vision can be viewed as a self-contained literary unit, it is clear from reading it that there is a chronology which is inherent to the text of the *Shepherd*. The *Visions* occur before Hermas has a chance to convey their contents and messages to his audience. The *Similitudes*, on the other hand, take place after this initial revelation. This is made evident from the fact that they speak of Hermas' actions regarding the *Visions* in the past tense. Similarly, *Similitudes* IX and X are necessarily the final parts of the story, as they state clearly that they occur after Hermas has had time to write down the preceding *Similitudes* (see *Sim* IX.1.1, X.1.1). The division which takes place at *Similitude* IX.1.1 may even mark the beginning of a third unique book, although documentary evidence does not show the unique circulation necessary to support this possibility.[25]

While the makeup of the *Shepherd* is interesting in its own right, it is the *genre* of the text which has sparked the most debate in the scholarly community. It is generally agreed upon that the best category for the *Shepherd* is that of an apocalypse. According to the SBL's Apocalypse Group,
"'Apocalypse' is a genre of revelatory literature with a narrative framework, in which a revelation is mediated by an otherworldly being to a human recipient, disclosing a transcendent reality which is both temporal, insofar as it envisages eschatological salvation, and spatial insofar as it involves another, supernatural world."[26]
It is easy to see from this definition why the generic classification of the *Shepherd* as an apocalypse is so popular. It takes place within a narrative framework, has otherworldly mediators, a human recipient, and aspects of a transcendent reality. However, it is the latter portion of the definition which gives the lie to such a classification, and scholars appear to be acutely aware of this fact. William Jardine subitles his translation of the *Shepherd* "The Gentle Apocalypse."[27] Osiek acknowledges that "The book lacks, or pays down considerably, some of what are often considered essential Elements of an apocalypse."[28] Ehrman states "there is some focus on the future course of human events... But even more the book deals

---

[25] See Bagnall, Roger S. 2009. *Early Christian Books in Egypt*. Princeton: Princeton University Press. 44ff for a more detailed discussion of the papyrological preservation of the *Shepherd*.

[26] Collins, John J. 1981. Apocalyptic Genre and Mythic Allusions in Daniel. *Journal For The Study Of The Old Testament*. 85

[27] 1992. Redwood City, CA: Proteus Publishing.

[28] *Commentary*. 11. She counters this by pointing out that there are other accepted apocalypses which lack one or more of these elements.

with problems of Christian existence in the here and now."[29] Holmes gives the most thorough treatment of this subject, establishing that it is only *Visions* I-IV which qualify as a Jewish-Hellenistic apocalypse (he likens the *Mandates* to homilies, and sees the *Similitudes* as simply that), and even then he acknowledges that "*Visions* 1-4 neatly reflect this pattern, **except for their contents**: the focus is not on the end, but on the possibility of repentance because the end is not yet."[30] (Emphasis added)

    The content of the *Shepherd* does contain certain aspects of apocalyptic content. In the *Mandates*, there is a recurring promise that someone who obeys the angel's commandments will "live to God." There is also a very brief discussion of the fate of sinners in the sixth *Similitude*. Additionally, there is the matter of second repentance, referenced above. These three elements could be said to represent the temporal transcendence and eschatological salvation necessary to classify the text as an apocalypse. However, even when taken together these three represent only a minority of the text, and two of the three are presented as having immediate significance rather than future relevance.

    In regards to a spatially transcendent reality, the evidence is even more weak. While Hermas does claim to be transported to other places on several occasions, the locations are all within the physical world with which he is familiar. Rather than being transported to another world or alternate reality to receive his visions, Hermas encounters his mediators on earth, and his visions are of mostly mundane things taking place in known areas.

    Collins has established that the SBL definition of Apocalypse "is not a random list of elements but a coherent structure, based on the systematic analysis of form and content."[31] The definition does not function as a set of diagnostic criteria of which a text must meet a certain number to qualify as an apocalypse. Rather, it establishes broad groupings of both *form* and *content* into

---

[29] Ehrman *Apostolic Fathers* 162

[30] Holmes, Michael W. 2007. *The Apostolic Fathers: Greek Texts and English Translations*. 3rd ed. Grand Rapids: Baker Academic. 445.

[31] Apocalyptic Genre. 85

which a text must fit. As there is near-universal acknowledgment that the content of the *Shepherd* does not truly qualify as an apocalyptic text. It may be said to take the apocalyptic form, but it does not truly fall into the apocalyptic genre.

Leaving aside apocalypse as a classification for the *Shepherd*, there is no other genre readily evident in which it could easily be placed. However, there are certain characteristics which hint at another way of viewing the text. As noted above, Holmes sees the *Mandates* as homiletical, and the *Similitudes* as allegorical similes, distinguishing them from the pseudo-apocalyptic text found in *Visions* I-IV. While this distinction seems logical on the surface, a closer analysis suggests that such a delineation is lacking in support from the text itself.

All three sections of the *Shepherd* contain angelic mediators as primary characters. The Shepherd character delivers the *Mandates* and the *Similitudes*, and the old woman mediates the *Visions*. So the aspect of an otherworldly mediator is equally spread among the three sections, and does not define the *Visions* as unique from the other two. We have already seen that the content does not fit the apocalyptic definition in any of the three sections, so this fails to make the *Visions* distinct as well. The remaining possibility is that the *Visions* are, as their common name suggests, a series of visions, while the others are not. But does this stand up to scrutiny? *Vision* II is only a vision insomuch as Hermas sees his mediators—something which is true for the *Mandates* and *Similitudes* as well. *Vision* I may qualify, in that Hermas has an encounter with someone he presumes to be dead, but one could argue that she is acting as a mediator. The only *Visions* which are distinctly visions, and not simple visits from mediators, are III and IV, with III being an extensive explanation of a detailed vision, and IV being a relatively short encounter with a supernatural being. However, these also do not distinguish this section from the others. *Vision* III, the most detailed of the four, is of a tower being built, and an explanation of its building. This is a theme which is repeated, and extensively expanded upon, in *Similitude* IX. *Similitudes* III and IV are both of trees, but one group of trees are enduring the hardships of winter, while the others are enjoying the bounty of summer. The narration reads as though Hermas is shown these two groups of trees without any apparent break in time, which would require at least one group to be a vision rather than real. *Similitudes* VI, VIII, and X also contain elements which are clearly supernatural (a punishing angel, an unrealistically large tree, and heavenly virgins, respectively). So then, the supernatural elements also do not distinguish the *Visions* from the *Similitudes*, and therefore there is no real reason to assume that they are different genres. Since Holmes sees no reason to classify the *Similitudes* as apocalyptic, he does not have much of a basis for doing so with the *Visions*, either. Both sections are most properly understood as groupings of allegorical similes, contained within a narrative structure.

Viewing the two outer sections as similes, and joining them together with the traditional homilies found in the *Mandates*, provides the basis for seeing the *Shepherd* as a part of a different genre—that of the homily. Following the example of Jesus, Hermas' work may very well be a collection of parables, diatribes, and other sayings meant to instruct and guide his community. In order to see this collection as homily, however, it must be more than simply a collection of that sort. In the following chapters, I will investigate the other components necessary to move from viewing the *Shepherd* as simply a collection of similes and diatribes, and toward seeing it as an example of early Christian homily.

Shea Zellweger

2 The Oral Nature of the *Shepherd*

The first characteristic necessary for the *Shepherd* to be viewed as homily is that of orality. Homilies are not written for literary consumption, but spoken aloud for an audience. In order for the *Shepherd* to be established as homily, then, it is necessary first to demonstrate its oral qualities. Carolyn Osiek has put forth an excellent review of the oral and literary characteristics of Hermas' world and writing,[32] and this chapter will follow her work closely. It will also engage eight of Walter Ong's nine characteristics of orality,[33] noting which of those characteristics exist with the *Shepherd*, and to what extent they are present. With the aid of these two sources, the oral qualities of the *Shepherd*, and the likelihood that it was a work intended to be heard and not read, will be firmly established.

I. Carolyn Osiek on the Orality of Hermas

In evaluating the level of literacy in Hermas' culture, Osiek observes that "the most sanguine estimates rarely reach 50

---

[32] 1998. The Oral World of Early Christianity in Rome: The Case of Hermas. In *Judaism and Christianity in First-Century Rome*. Grand Rapids: Wm. B Eerdmans Publishing Co.

[33] 1982 *Orality and Literacy: The Technologizing of the Word*. London and New York: Methuen. 37-57

percent,"[34] but also notes others' estimations for the Christian population at 10-15 percent, and ultimately concludes that when it came to the highest level of literacy, "the ability to compose literary works or to think habitually in ways associated with literacy. The percentage of the population that did think habitually in those ways must have been very small indeed."[35] This, of course, speaks not to the likelihood of Hermas' level of literacy—the fact that he wrote the *Shepherd* is clear evidence that he was entirely literate—but to the likelihood that he would have used literature to communicate with his community. If more than half of his audience could not read at all, and less than 10 percent had any advanced literary abilities, it is not likely that the written word would have been the medium of choice for a message intended for his house church, or for the community as a whole.

Osiek then turns to the content of the text itself, and illustrates clearly the emphasis it places on oral communication.[36] The instruction Hermas receives is itself recorded as oral communication from his mediators, while the written word plays a much smaller role in the course of the story. In *Vision* I, his mediator reads aloud to him, transforming written communication into oral proclamation (perhaps a foreshadowing of what is to be done with the text Hermas has written). In *Vision* II, Hermas is presented with a book, the contents of which are preserved in *Vision* II.2.2-3.4. Despite its brevity, the book takes Hermas two weeks to read and understand, while the visions and oral communications he receives and interacts with are questioned, evaluated, and comprehended on the spot. "Only in 5.5, under the direction of the newly appeared shepherd, does writing reenter the narrative, this time again as oral dictation, for the purpose not of private reading but of oral proclamation."[37] As with the lady reading aloud to Hermas, this dictation cannot truly be understood as literary in its scope, but as a written preservation of oral

---

[34] Osiek, Oral World. 159

[35] Ibid. 160

[36] Ibid.

[37] Ibid.

communication. Hermas is to write what he hears, so that his audience can hear what he writes, thereby making the text a temporary carrier of a spoken message, and not a written message in its own right.

There are, however, traces of literary quality intrinsic to the text of the *Shepherd*. Osiek notes in particular the use of itemized lists, which she identifies as "a primary use of literacy."[38] She identifies several other structures, such as structured chiasms, which may represent the literary quality of the text, but are also possible in orality, and so should not be viewed as clear evidence for either. Osiek further acknowledges that a "linear, logical reading of the text reveals many inconsistencies."[39] This should not be seen as evidence of multiple authorship, but rather of orality: "In the process of oral proclamation, the coherence of the immediate subject with the life world of the hearers is the focus, not overall coherence with all the images and narratives presented."[40]

A distinction offered by Osiek which sets Hermas apart from other studies of oral literature is worth noting. While the text is narrative in its form, its content is intended primarily as instruction, setting it apart from the epic poetry and narrative which is usually the subject of such studies. Because of this distinction, "we have in this text evidence for the oral formulation not of narrative but of paraenetic material, within an apocalyptic framework."[41] This offers the possibility of the *Shepherd* as a (mostly complete) paraenetic outline which would be used as the basis for oral instruction, rather than simply as a narrative intended for oral performance.

II. Walter Ong's Eight Characteristics of Orally Based Thought and Expression

While Osiek devotes several pages to a brief outline of how Hermas exhibits the majority of these characteristics,[42] it is necessary for the purpose of this study to review each characteristic, and its relation to the text of the *Shepherd*. It should be noted that the

---

[38] Ibid. 162

[39] Ibid. 171

[40] Ibid.

[41] Ibid.

[42] Ibid. See p163-168

Shepherd, as a written document, cannot qualify under Ong's classification of a primary oral culture, which is "totally untouched by any knowledge of writing or print."[43] Any evidence of orality must be seen as evidence of the degree to which Hermas' writing preserves the oral mindset. While Ong lists nine characteristics, only eight of them can be closely examined for the purpose of a written work. The final category addresses the difference in mindset between primary oral and secondary oral cultures. Ong establishes clearly that even a little bit of schooling in literacy is sufficient to counteract the ninth characteristic,[44] so a totally literate person such as Hermas could not reasonably be expected to still have it.

I. *Additive rather than subordinative*[45]

As Hermas describes the twelve mountains shown to him by the Shepherd in *Similitude* IX.1, he introduces each mountain with a formulaic "τὸ δὲ." This repetitive "and the" is a hallmark of additive language. Translators tasked with rendering the text readable for a secondary oral culture such as ours are content to suppress the use of "and," using multiple synonyms or excluding it entirely, as such repetition would seem strange to us. Yet it is perfectly natural for Hermas to say, and likely would have been natural for his audience to hear. And this is but one example of the use of additive language in the text of the *Shepherd*.

When Hermas questions his mediators about various aspects of the visions they show him, there is no clear pattern of movement from specific to general, or vice versa. Hermas may ask a question which follows logically from the preceding question and answer, or it may be a complete non sequitor, without any apparent acknowledgment that the subject is being changed. The same is true of their explanations, which can move from answering a stated question, to explaining some other aspect of the vision, with no concluding or introductory statements to separate one from the other.

In Hermas' vision of the tower in *Vision* III, the woman church gives an extensive explanation of what the various stones

---

[43] Ong, *Orality and Literacy*. 11

[44] Ibid. 51

[45] Ibid. 37

signify, and it is stated in no uncertain terms in III.7.4 that she has completed this explanation. Yet Hermas follows this completion with a request for further explanation about another aspect of the tower, and receives one, which Osiek notes is a very different type of explanation than those which preceded it.[46] This paratactic connection, and the fact that the latter explanation is not in any way subordinate to the former, is a further indication that Hermas' work utilizes additive structures.

II. Aggregative rather than Analytic[47]

Four times in the course of just two verses in *Vision* II, Hermas feels compelled to refer to the woman church as old. Twice, he does so by referring to her as "την πρεσβυτεραν," and twice with the adjectival "πρεσβυτερα." This is restated a few lines later in *Vision* III.1, and in III.103 Hermas once again emphasizes just how old the woman appeared to be, this time in contrast to her appearance in *Visions* II and III which, we learn, was different than in the first *Vision*, which is the only one in which she truly appeared old. This need to frequently refer to her not simply as a woman, but as an *old* woman, is an example of Hermas' use of aggregative language. In a similar vein, when Hermas' mediators address him, they tend to use one of several adjectives. Depending on the circumstances, Hermas may be double-minded, foolish, bold, or self-controlled, but rarely is he simply "Hermas," with no qualifying adjective. Christians, meanwhile, are routinely referred to as οι δουλοι του θεου (in more than thirty contexts, by Osiek's reckoning[48]), giving the audience a title with which to refer to themselves.

Formulaic language, a close relative of aggregative speech, is employed to remind the audience of the purpose of the commands given. The majority of the *Mandates*, as well as several of the *Similitudes*, contain promises that those who heed what the Shepherd says will "live to God." Other formulae occur in multiple times in short, localized bursts, offering the listener a recurring refrain for an individual context.

---

[46] Oral World. 163

[47] Ong, *Orality and Literacy*. 38

[48] Oral World, 164

III. Redundant or 'copious.[49]

"Redundancy, repetition of the just-said, keeps both speaker and hearer surely on track."[50] The formulaic language and frequent repetition of adjectives and titles mentioned under the second characteristic are but a couple examples of Hermas' use of redundancy in his approach to writing. The bulk of the text deals in metaphor and explanation as a paraenetic method. This is a common approach, and is seen regularly in contemporary speech and writing. But what sets the oral characteristics of Hermas apart from any modern counterparts is the level of redundancy used. *Similitudes* VIII and IX, for instance, describe in great detail the various aspects of a willow tree and a tower, respectively. Hermas then commences to ask the Shepherd about each individual part of the structure in question, apparently not wanting to miss anything. This becomes tedious for a modern audience, as Hermas takes the time to ask about each group of sticks or stones in between two extremes, and the answers yield the results that one would have expected, being already aware of what the two extremes represented. A secondary oral author would assume that his or her reader would only need the two extremes, perhaps with one example of an in-between state, and would be able to reason out what the remainder represented. Not so for the residually oral text, which still operates like the spoken word, using devices to insure that the audience will remember what was said, rather than relying on its preservation in the body of the text. As Osiek describes it,

> "In the *Shepherd*, most of the explanations are wordy and expansive, often to the point of being tedious to the modern reader. The paraenetic sections of the *Mandates* are repetitive, often because the interlocutor Hermas has asked for further explanation, a device that both engages the hearer and provides the occasion to add material."

IV Conservative or traditionalist.[51]

Hermas' work is only partially conservative in its approach. There is very little in the way of quoting authoritative sources, and

---

[49] Ong, *Orality and Literacy.* 39

[50] Ibid. 40

[51] Ibid. 41

the use of mnemonic devices appears to be mostly limited to the aggregative and formulaic tactics mentioned above.[52] However, there is very much a traditionalist leaning in the information which Hermas presents. As Ong notes, the need to preserve what has been learned in an oral culture "establishes a highly traditionalist or conservative set of mind that with good reason inhibits intellectual experimentation."[53] This mindset is evident in Hermas' presentation of apparently new information. A large majority of the text is dedicated to information which would likely have been accepted as known by his community. But worked carefully into the old information is his new proposal; that repentance can occur after baptism. While the new information is not, in itself, traditionalist, the presentation format is carefully constructed to make it amicable to the traditionalist mindset. Hermas presents this knowledge as authoritative because it comes from a heavenly source, and repeats it several times to make sure the audience will grasp it. He also places it in the middle of the work, thereby surrounding it with accepted knowledge and making it innocuous. If it had been in his opening lines, he likely would have lost his audience right away. If, on the other hand, it had been his conclusion, it would have been the last thing his listeners heard, and the thing which they were most likely to question. By setting it in the middle of accepted information, Hermas avoided both of these pitfalls, and increased the likelihood that his audience would accept this new information. This careful placement, use of a divine source, and repetition of the point, works to insure that the audience will remember this new information, and remember it in such a way that it will remain in their minds as true.

V Close to the human lifeworld[54]

Here we see the influence that literacy has had on Hermas, yet at the same time the residual impact of orality on his writing. The *Shepherd* contains multiple lists, which Ong identifies as a characteristic of literacy, asserting that "an oral culture has no

---

[52] At least insofar as we have sources to which we can compare the *Shepherd*. It is possible that he makes regular use of phrases and mnemonics familiar to his community, but lost to us.

[53] Ibid.

[54] Ibid. 42

vehicle so neutral as a list."⁵⁵ At the same time, Hermas' description of various groups of people and objects exhibit this closeness to the human lifeworld. He does not list them in any itemized fashion, but describes them in regard to their actions and relationships. The ninth *Similitude* again provides a good example; when Hermas inquires as to the identity of a group of virgins, the Shepherd takes several sections to explain their deeds and abilities before finally presenting their names, and even at that juncture he identifies them not just by name, but by their level of power relative to one another as well.

VI Agonistically toned[56]

There is very little in the way of internal reflection in the *Shepherd*. On the few instances when Hermas informs his audience that he was engaged in some inner turmoil, the subject matter of the turmoil is not breached until a dialog partner is present. Throughout the dialogs themselves, there is a consistent pattern of praise and debasement inherent to residual orality. Hermas is careful to be intentionally humble in the presence of his mediators, and they are unabashed in decrying his apparently negative traits, or lauding his positive ones. Unlike an epic, where the hero might engage in verbal sparring with an opponent to gain the upper hand, it is clear that Hermas and his mediators acknowledge that they are superior to him, and act accordingly. Yet they all still speak in ways that reinforce his inferiority to his angelic companions.

The *Mandates* and some of the *Similitudes* provide another source of agonistic language, in the form of a classic "two ways" dialog. In the *Mandates*, it is a discussion between two things, one which leads to evil, and the other to good. In the *Similitudes*, the discussion is personified, most notably by the contrast of the virgins in the ninth *Similitude* to the wicked women. Rather than establishing good and allowing his audience to reason out that the opposite would be evil, Hermas pits good and evil against one another in agonistic fashion.

VII Empathetic and participatory rather than objectively distanced[57]

---

[55] Ibid.

[56] Ibid. 43

[57] Ibid. 45

Because Hermas chose to make himself the primary protagonist of his narrative, it is difficult to quantify the extent to which his work is characterized by empathy and participation. He cannot inject himself into the story on occasion to address the characters, because he is already present as one of the characters. However, it seems readily apparent that the goal of the work is a broader participation on the part of the hearers, which cannot be measured directly from the script. As suggested in chapter one, it is likely that Hermas' family in the narrative serves as a surrogate for his community, and therefore offers an opportunity for them to participate in the story. He also directly addresses his brethren multiple times during the *Visions*, further encouraging their participation in the course of the narrative. This may also be an example of how paraenetic narrative differs from epic narrative in an oral culture, as it is the audience that is called to insert itself into the story, rather than the narrator inserting him or herself as representative of the whole community.

VIII Homeostatic[58]

"[O]ral societies live very much in a present which keeps itself in equilibrium or homeostasis by sloughing off memories which no longer have present relevance."[59] Hermas' explanations of the various metaphors, images, and symbols present in the *Shepherd* can be immensely confusing to a secondary oral culture accustomed to careful delineation and fixed categories. The inclination of the literate to track symbols and assume that they have the same meaning will quickly be lost in the primary oral realm. For instance, Hermas identifies the woman mediator as the church, but in *Vision* III states that the tower is the church. In *Similitude IX*, the tower is revisited, but this time it is the Son of God, who is also the gate in the tower. In *Vision* V, the "son of God" is a title given to the Holy Spirit, while a character who is presumably Jesus is the adopted son of God. The primary oral audience is willing to accept these changes, not requiring earlier memories to be in harmony with the new image.

---

[58] Ibid. 46

[59] Ibid.

Osiek also points out the focus of the *Shepherd* on the temporal present: "For example, Hermas tries to establish with the Shepherd a schema of the duration of punishment for those who live in heedless luxury (*Sim.* 6.4.5), but exactness keeps eluding him. Punishment endures for equal time (4.1), a short time (4.3), but has the force of a ratio of real time (4.4). Eventually it becomes clear that the Shepherd is not talking about duration of time at all, but making the psychological observation that pleasure has a short memory and suffering a long one (5.3-4)."[60]

Together, Osiek and Ong offer a reasonable basis for the *Shepherd* to be seen as oral literature. Ong's characterization of orality demonstrates clearly that Hermas wrote from a position of high residual orality. We know that literature with a high degree of technical proficiency was being composed at the time that Hermas wrote, so it is very likely that this residual orality is a result of Hermas' intent for the work to be spoken. Osiek's evaluation of the *Shepherd*, and in particular its tendency to emphasize the spoken word while diminishing the role of text, also provides strong evidence that it was Hermas' intent that his work would be heard by its audience, rather than read.

Having demonstrated the oral qualities of the *Shepherd*, there are still other qualifications necessary to classify the text in my proposed genre of homily. In the following chapter, these qualifications will be identified, and the extent to which the *Shepherd* meets them will be investigated.

---

[60] Oral World, 168

3 The *Shepherd* as Homily

In the previous chapter, the oral qualities of the *Shepherd* were established; demonstrating that the work is most likely a textual preservation of what was originally an oral presentation. However, the orality of the text does not, in and of itself, prove that it is in fact homiletical in nature. Homiletics is a sub-genre of oral material, so further evidence is necessary to move from recognizing the *Shepherd* as simply oral, to understanding it as specifically homiletical. In this chapter, I will present several portions of the text which provide this evidence.

In order to categorize something as homily, it is first necessary to determine what such a categorization means. Several authors have attempted to create a classification system by which to distinguish homily from other forms of speech, as well as from other forms of religious texts. McDonald, for instance, offers four categories; *Propheteia, paraklēsis, paraenesis,* and *paradosis,* and places homiletics under the category of *paraklēsis*[61]. As Stewart-Sykes notes, "this model is operational and as such does not intend to answer the form-critical question of how the homilies of the

---

[61] McDonald, James I. H. 1980. *Kerygma and Didache.* Edited by R. M. Wilson, *Society for New Testament Studies Monograph Series.* New York: Cambridge University Press. 11-12

earliest Christians might be discovered."[62] Such a categorization, then, is not particularly useful when discovering early Christian homily is our goal. However, other authors have offered definitions which are useful to this end. Stewart-Sykes provides an extensive evaluation of what may or may not be homily, but ultimately he recognizes that what the forms of homily have in common "is a deep dependence on the scriptural text."[63] McClure, writing in regard to the things necessary to formulate a homily, makes the use of Scripture one of the "four rhetorical codes [which] are fundamental to preaching."[64] In addition to being based upon Scripture, it is implicit within the work of both McClure and Stewart-Sykes that the homily is an oral communication, separating it from written communications which were also based on Scripture.

These definitions are at the same time helpful and anachronistic when evaluating the *Shepherd*. Stewart-Sykes' evaluation is primarily in the context of Jewish homily as a basis for Christian homily.[65] Jews of Late Antiquity had a broad range of religious texts which were generally understood as Scripture. Likewise McClure, writing for a contemporary audience, does so with the understanding that his readers are aware of those Christian religious texts which have been codified and canonized as Scripture. Writing at the turn of the second century, Hermas would not have had the benefit of an agreed upon canon, and in all likelihood his church would have still been relying as heavily upon oral tradition as they did upon textual tradition, if not more so. Even attempting to

---

[62] 2001. *From Prophecy to Preaching* Vol. LIX, *Supplements to Vigiliae Christianae*. Leiden, the Netherlands: Koninklijke Brill. 27

[63] Ibid. 57

[64] McClure, John S. *The Four Codes of Preaching*. Minneapolis: Augsburg Fortress Press, 1991. 9

[65] Beginning on page 40 of *Prophecy to Preaching*, Stewart-Sykes details the "proem form," a diatribe-type speech consisting of five parts, as an early form of Jewish homily which may have subsequently been adopted by early Christians. He offers a brief presentation of other Jewish homiletic forms on pages 52-56.

use the term "Scripture" when discussing Christians in this time period belies how malleable their use of religious texts would have been.

An adequate definition of homiletics as it relates to the *Shepherd* will necessarily have to take into account these differences in religious context. So, rather than understanding a homily in Hermas' time as an oral presentation with a "deep dependence on the scriptural text," I offer this new, somewhat adapted, definition: *A Christian homily at the turn of the 2nd century CE was an oral presentation which depends directly upon some text or oral tradition which was esteemed by the audience as beneficial for religious instruction.*

Clearly, this definition comes with its share of obstacles. It is impossible to present evidence for a first- or second- century oral tradition without having some textual preservation thereof. It is likewise impossible to present evidence for a textual dependence without explicit citation or an extant copy of the text in question. So, while the definition is apropos to the time period in theory, a contemporary analysis will need textual evidence in practice. The reality of the orality of Antiquity does, however, remind us that the text where a tradition is preserved might not have been accessed by the homiletician. With this definition, and its limitation, in mind, I now turn to the *Shepherd* of Hermas.

In 1905, a study of the New Testament's presence in the Apostolic Fathers concluded, in part, that "The author of the Shepherd of Hermas nowhere supplies us with a direct quotation from the Old or New Testament, and we are therefore obliged to fall back upon allusions which always admit of some degree of doubt."[66] The study then classified suspected allusions by likelihood of reliance A-D,[67] with few receiving higher than a C. These decisions must, however, be taken for what they are: The purpose of the study was to determine textual dependence based on similarity

---

[66] The New Testament in the Apostolic Fathers. 1905. 105

[67] A= 'no reasonable doubt; B= 'a high degree of probability'; C= 'a lower degree of probability; D= 'too uncertain to allow any reliance.' Other possible allusions were mentioned but not classified, presumably because their probability of reliance was below that of the D class.

of word choice, something which is more a marker of literary relationships than oral ones. Additionally, the findings of the study are the consensus of multiple scholars. Individually, the likelihood of any allusion may have held greater weight with some scholars than others, and the final consensus would have reflected a lower level of certainty. Finally, the conclusions of the study have come under scrutiny in recent years. John Muddiman notes "Although some of the committee's assessments are questionable... the importance of this refinement of criteria and careful distinctions as to degrees of probability was an important advance in critical scholarship."[68]

I. *Hermas* and *Ephesians*

One connection that the committee deemed particularly high was that between the *Shepherd* and the *Epistle to the Ephesians*. Two passages in the *Shepherd* were classified as having a 'b' grade relationship to *Ephesians*,[69] and several other allusions are given 'c' and 'd' level connections. This is sufficient evidence to suggest a strong probability of connection between the two texts, and even to bolster the claim of some relationships which were graded lower. One such relationship is between *Vision* III and *Ephesians* 2:10-22, which is the first of three potential homilies to be examined in this chapter.

The primary image of the *Vision* is of a tower being built on a foundation of water. The stones being used to build the tower are Christians, making the tower itself an implicit representation of the Church, although the author does not choose to make this explicit, perhaps because it would conflict with the revelation he receives after the third *Vision* that his female mediator represents the Church as well. Whatever his reason for leaving the fact unspoken, it is clear that this tower is meant to represent the members of the Jesus movement.

---

[68] 2005. The Church in Ephesians, 2 Clement, and the *Shepherd of Hermas*. In *Trajectories through the New Testament and Apostolic Fathers* New York: Oxford University Press. 107

[69] The New Testament in the Apostolic Fathers. 1905. 106

Another differentiation from the pattern of the *Ephesians* passage is found in the placement of the apostles. While *Ephesians* 2:20 states that the building is "ἐποικοδομηθέντες ἐπὶ τῷ θεμελίῳ τῶν ἀποστόλων καὶ προφητῶν, ὄντος ἀκρογωνιαίου αὐτοῦ Χριστοῦ Ἰησοῦ," Hermas' tower is built on a foundation of water, meant to represent baptism, and the Apostles have been relocated so that they, along with the prophets, "συμφωνοῦντες ταῖς ἁρμογαῖσ αὐτῶν."[70] Serving as a cornerstone is clearly intended to be a place of honor, as evidenced by both the *Vision* and the *Ephesians* passage, so it is clear that Hermas intends for the Apostles to retain a position of honor, even as he attempts to make a case for baptism as foundational to Christian faith. But perhaps the most glaring difference here is that Christ is absent from Hermas' image. This is a significant departure, and it should not be ignored. However, Hermas' Christology is underdeveloped, even for its time period, so neither should there be excessive significance attached to this apparent oversight.

One possible explanation for the absence of Christ from the tower lies in the definition of "chief cornerstone." In Ephesians, the term used is "ἀκρογωνιαίου." Reference to Jesus as the "chief cornerstone" is, however, very common in the New Testament, being found in the Gospels, Acts, and 1 Peter, and having its origin in the Psalms. We can therefore conclude that the term was likely a familiar one to 2nd Century Christians. Many extant manuscripts use the term "κεφαλὴν γωνίας,"[71] which would make Jesus the stone which is at the head (or top) of the corner. *Vision* III.8.9 emphasizes the fact that the tower has not been completed at the time Hermas is seeing it, making it possible that he merged the more common "κεφαλὴν γωνίας" with the "ἀκρογωνιαίου" of *Ephesians*, and concluded that until the tower had been completed, Christ should be absent from it.

That Hermas sees Christ as an integral part of the church is confirmed by *Similitude* IX, which also presents the Church as a tower. This second tower is built on a rock, with a large gate, which the Shepherd informs Hermas are both representations of the Son

---

[70] *Vision* III.5.1

[71] See *Matthew* 21:42, among others.

of God.⁷² The Son of God is also the one who commissioned the tower, and it is by his powers that the tower is built.⁷³ In this image, the apostles are still able to serve as a source of foundation, atop the first and second generations of "upright men" (ανδρων δικαιων), and the prophets, which are built , each on top of the other, on the foundation of the Son of God.⁷⁴

We see in each of these tower stories a reminiscence of the concepts in Ephesians, but no clear quotation. This is not surprising, as the 1905 study noted that "it is not the way of Hermas to quote, but to take suggestions, and alter to suit his own purposes."⁷⁵ However, together they make a compelling case that Hermas has in his mind an image of the church as a building, with the apostles, prophets, and Christ as integral parts in its construction, all of which is also found in *Ephesians*.

Another point of connection between the *Shepherd* and *Ephesians* is found in the image of the church as transcendent and pre-existent. Muddiman, while doubting the textual links found by the 1905 study, attempts to demonstrate that "the similarities in the concept of the transcendent church between these three texts is very striking."⁷⁶ He further contends

> "that Christians are already raised and seated in the heavenly
> realms is the most striking expression of the realized
> eschatology of Ephesians... Ephesians is nearer to the *Shepherd*
> in applying it to a present possibility for the Christian, all the
> necessary qualifications notwithstanding."⁷⁷

Muddiman is more convinced of this latter relationship than that between the *Ephesians* 2 and the two building metaphors in the *Shepherd*, but ultimately his position affirms a relationship between the two texts, possibly by way of *2 Clement*. While he might see his

---

⁷² *Similitude* IX.12.1

⁷³ *Similitude* IX.12.8, IX.13.2

⁷⁴ *Similitude* IX.15.4

⁷⁵ The New Testament in the Apostolic Fathers. 106

⁷⁶ Muddiman, John. 2005. The Church in Ephesians. 121 The third text referenced in the quotation is *2 Clement*.

⁷⁷ Ibid. 120

differentiation as a point of contention between himself and the authors of the 1905 study, it still provides further confirmation of some relationship between the two texts in question.

The presentation of the Lady Church in the *Shepherd* offers further connection *Ephesians*. *Vision* III.10.2-13.4 recounts the gradual change in appearance of the lady, from old and frail to young and beautiful, which the Shepherd informs Hermas is due to his own spiritual growth, from being of two minds to courage in the Lord. Hermas, as a member and representative of the Church, helps her to become beautiful and to shed her wrinkle by becoming holy. While there are no verbal parallels to *Ephesians* 5:25-27, the subject matter is very similar. Muddiman contributes here as well:

> "Eph. 5:27 refers to the preparation of the bride-church for union with Christ as the washing away not, as one might expect, of the dirt of sin, but of every disfiguring skin blemish (σπίλος) or wrinkle/sign of ageing (πυτίσ). Whether the author consciously intended by this unusual imagery a reference to baptismal rejuvenation (see John 3. 5), it was open to someone like Hermas to pick up and extensively develop the image in his visions of the woman-church gradually becoming younger in appearance."[78]

This similarity, in addition to the fact that the potential reference is found within the greater context of *Vision* III, one of the two sources of Church-tower imagery, is sufficient to make plain the case for a relationship between *Vision* III and *Ephesians*.

There are also smaller hinted parallels throughout the ninth *Similitude* which might provide further connection to *Ephesians*. *Similitude* IX.17, for instance, says the stones which build the church come from twelve mountains which represent the twelve nations of the world, possibly echoing *Ephesians* 2:19's assertion that some who are built into the tower were formerly "ξένοι καὶ πάροικοι." Likewise, the need for some of the stones to be hewn (ελατομησεν)[79] might be a veiled reference to the conflict of circumcision in *Ephesians*2:13. Finally, *Similitude* IX.17.4 contains a creedal formula asserting that those who receive the seal of Christ have "μίαν φρόνησιν ἔσχον και ἕνα νουν, καί μία πίστις αὐτῶν ἐγένετο καί μία ἀγάπη," offering a parallel to *Ephesians* 4:4-6's "ἓν

---

[78] Ibid. 112.

[79] *Similitude* IX.9.3

σῶμα καὶ ἓν πνεῦμα ... εἷς κύριος, μία πίστις, ἓν βάπτισμα. εἷς θεὸς καὶ πατὴρ πάντων."

Each of these parallels falls short in being conclusive on its own merits alone. However, when put together they build a strong case for a relationship of some kind. That two authors, independently of one another, would offer this amount of similar imagery, theology, and creedal commitment in proximity to one another, is improbable to say the least. While we should be careful to conclude definite direct dependence from one to the other, it is evident that the two texts have some connection, be that direct dependence, indirect dependence, or a mutual dependence on some unknown source or tradition.

II. *Similitude* V and the New Testament

The fifth *Similitude* offers several possible New Testament Parallels. The central parable recounts the story of a master who commissions a slave to fence in one of his vineyards, and subsequently rewards the slave for doing more than was asked of him. In establishing the premise of the parable, Hermas recalls two known Jesus parables, one more distinctly than the other.

First, there is a possible intersection between *Similitude* V and *Luke* 13:6-9. Per usual, there is minimal linguistic connection between the two parables. Each contain the word vineyard (ἀμπελῶνι) and the future, active, first-person singular use of the verb "to dig" (σκάψω), but these words are common enough, and their usage in the parables distinct enough, that there is no real linguistic evidence for a literary connection. Second, there are slight parallels to the parable of the tenants in *Matthew* 21:33-41.[80] The faint connections are found in similarities like the owner of a vineyard leaving it in the care of others, and subsequently his decision to go away on a journey (ἀπεδήμησεν). But again, the linguistic correlations are not enough in their own right to merit a claim for literary relationship.

In order to establish such a relationship, then, there must be some other standard presented. Albert Bates Lord provides such a standard in his work on oral poetry. His observation of oral poets in the former Yugoslavia produced a concept of *themes* in oral work,

---

[80] Also *Mark* 12:1-2, *Luke* 20:9-19

defined as "the groups of ideas regularly used in telling a tale in the formulaic style of traditional song."[81] These themes are distinguished from the more specific *formula* of Milman Parry, which is a "group of words which is regularly employed under the same metrical conditions to express a given essential idea."[82] Themes do not require identical formulae, nor do they need to be placed in a specific order. In fact, Davis observes that the combinations of themes in new ways "can result in inconsistencies where two themes are brought together without meshing the facts of the two situations."[83] He further notes that

> "Singers may vary their telling of a story by the use of elaboration or simplification, expansion of ornamentation, changes of order in the sequence, addition of material not in a given text but found in the texts of singers from other districts, omission of material and 'substitution of one theme for another, in a story held together by inner tension.'"

Given that it is commonly accepted that the authors of the Gospels altered parables in order to better convey their individual messages,[84] I would offer a similar evaluation of the telling and preservation of Jesus' parables. Tellers utilized all of these techniques in their attempts to use Jesus' parables as a basis for conveying their intended message. If this is the case, and Jesus' parables can be evaluated on a rubric similar to that of Yugoslavian singers, we should expect to find a collection of themes which provide continuity between many of the parables. I contend that such a collection of themes exist. Furthermore, there are multiple themes which are prevalent in the Jesus parable tradition, and several can also be found in *Similitude* V. Among these themes are:

---

[81] 1960. *The singer of tales, Harvard studies in comparative literature ; 24.* Cambridge: Harvard University Press. 69

[82] 1930. Studies in the epic technique of oral verse-making. I. Homer and the Homeric Style. *Harvard Studies in Classical Philology* 41:73-147. 80

[83] 1999. Oral Biblical Criticism. *Journal for the Study of the New Testament Supplement Series* 172. 13

[84] See, for instance, *Matthew* 25:14-30's interpretation of a *Q* source parable as compared to that of *Luke* 19:11-27.

- A property owner placing his possessions in the care of others (*Matt.* 21:33-43 and parallels, *Luke* 19:11-27 and parallels, *Mark* 13:33-37 and parallels, *Luke* 13:6-9)
- A master instructs people to work in a vineyard (*Matt.* 20:1-16 and parallels, *Matt.* 21:33-43 and parallels, *Matt.* 21:28-31, *Luke* 13:6-9)
- A person receives instruction and does something other than he was asked (Luke 14:15-24 and parallels, *Matt.* 21:33-43 and parallels, *Matt.* 21:28-31, *Luke* 13:6-9)
- A servant's actions are rewarded unfairly (*Matt.* 20:1-16 and parallels, *Matt.* 25:14-30 and parallels, *Luke* 16:1-8)

This is by no means an exhaustive list of themes, either in the Jesus parable tradition, or in *Similitude* V. However, these four themes combine to form the basic structure of the *Similitude*. On the whole, the books of *Matthew* and *Luke* appear to bear the strongest witness to the four themes in question, providing a possible connection to *Q*, but each of the synoptic Gospels—as well as the *Gospel of Thomas*—contains them in some form, so any of them could represent the tradition upon which Hermas is relying. We can, then, tentatively say that this parable shows evidence of being related to the oral tradition surrounding the parables of Jesus in general.

I contend further that its specific content bears enough thematic similarity to *Luke* 13:6-9 to merit consideration for a direct relationship between the two stories. There is clearly a different focus in *Similitude* V than in the *Luke* passage; while Luke makes the story a standalone parable with no clear ending and eschatological significance, Hermas uses it as the beginning of a longer narrative with a Christological focus. This is reminiscent of Hermas' treatment of *Ephesians*, in which a brief statement on the part of the source is expanded into a lengthy discourse, often only tangentially related to the original statement.[85]

---

[85] This may provide a measure of confirmation to Stewart-Sykes' aforementioned thesis that early Christian preaching was adapted from the Jewish proem form of diatribe, which will be examined further below.

The expanded portion of the parable, and its subsequent explanation, also show a possible thematic connection to an extant text. *Similitude* V.2.2-9 and V.5.1-6.8 recount and explain (respectively) the actions of the servant, the reward for his work, and the theological significance thereof. The servant, who is intended to represent the Son of God, goes beyond what his master requires so, in addition to the promised reward, he is made joint-heir with the master's true son. The work the servant did is said to represent the Son of God "clean[sing] the sins of the people."[86] This story bears a remarkable thematic similarity to *Philippians* 2:7b-11, the majority of a passage otherwise known as the *Kenosis Hymn*. Someone bearing the nature of a servant surpasses perfection in obedience, and is subsequently elevated to a new position and given a new name, with the rest of those involved giving their affirmation of his new station. The only portion of the *Kenosis Hymn* which does not have its parallel in the parable is the opening statement "ὅς ἐν μορφῇ θεοῦ ὑπάρχων οὐχ ἁρπαγμὸν ἡγήσατο τὸ εἶναι ἴσα θεῷ."[87] Hermas apparently anticipates this issue, and while he is not able to adjust the parable accordingly, he makes provision for it in the explanation thereof. *Similitude* V.6.1-2 informs us that "εἰσ δούλου τρόπον οὐ κειται ὁ υἱός του θεου, ἀλλ' εἰσ ἐξουςίαν μεγάλην κειται καί κυριότητα... τόν λαόν ἔκτυτε καί παρέδωκε το₁ υἱω₁ αὐτων." This rationale is confusing, and does not appear to truly fit the rest of the story, but in offering it, Hermas is able to cover every aspect of the *Kenosis Hymn*. This intentional inclusion of so awkward an explanation, which manages to fully sync the story with the hymn, is too convenient to be entirely coincidental.

The *Kenosis Hymn* also bears the distinction of being a pre-existing oral tradition which Paul incorporated into the text of *Philippians*.[88] If the epistle was, in fact, written in Rome as it claims,[89] we have a basis for assuming that the hymn was being sung by

---

[86] *Similitude* V.6.3

[87] *Philippians* 2:6

[88] Davis, Casey Wayne. Oral Biblical Criticism 114

[89] The reference to the palace guard in, 1:13, coupled with the greeting from Caesar's household in 4:22, leave little room for an alternative setting.

Christians of that region. It is then likely that Hermas, as a Roman Christian, would have been familiar with the hymn through oral tradition, independently of any familiarity with *Philippians*. Additionally, his Roman audience's acquaintance with the hymn would have made it a prime source after which to pattern a homily.

Between its connection to the Jesus parable tradition, and its thematic and structural similarities to the *Kenosis Hymn*, *Similitude* V shows strong potential for being a homily based on traditions which Hermas and his community considered sacred. Since we only have thematic evidence, and no precise formulaic intersections, neither relationship is beyond doubt.[90] Still, each lends further substance to the theory that Hermas wrote the *Shepherd* homiletically.

III. Other claims of textual relationships.

Several authors have suggested additional possibilities for literary relationships between the *Shepherd* and other Christian texts. Most notable among this are Aune, Stewart-Sykes, and Osiek. Each author is careful not to speak with certainty, or to necessarily accept the relationships proposed by others. However, between the three they make a compelling case.

Osiek, writing in her commentary, offers a series of potential literary connections. She begins by emphasizing that "Any similarity between parables in *Hermas* and those in the Gospels is better explained on the basis of a common oral tradition."[91] The likelihood of a common oral tradition rather than a direct textual influence should not, however, deter us from seeing potential for homily, as per the proposed definition above. Following this caveat, she offers slight similarities between the *Shepherd* and *1 Thessalonians* and *John*, and a more general commonality with the Synoptic tradition and Paul concerning the nature of the Kingdom of God.[92] These are

---

[90] Using the same classification scale as the aforementioned 1905 study, the highest either correlation could be rated is a B, yet at the same time I posit that they are thematically similar enough to merit no less than a C.

[91] 1999. *Commentary* 26

[92] Ibid.

all simple and incidental connections. However she also proposes two, more substantial, interactions.

"Similarities with the letter of James abound," Osiek writes, "and here the relationship is considerably more complex."[93] She begins by addressing the two texts' common usage of the "double-minded" (δίψυχος), though she is quick to point out that the word appears only twice in *James*, and one of those instances does not carry the same inflected meaning portrayed in the *Shepherd*.

> "Another similarity is that both James and *Hermas* have a deep concern for the poor and needy and a mistrust of the rich, but in *Hermas* the mistrust of the rich is tempered by reminder and exhortation to their responsibility (*Vis* 3.9; *Man.* 2.3; *Sim.* 2), whereas in James the condemnation of the rich is never compromised by a suggestion that they are important to the community."[94]

Again, the similarity is in some manner offset by departure, but as we have seen above this is not uncommon, either internally among the New Testament authors, or in Hermas' use thereof. The final substantial connection between *James* and the *Shepherd* offered by Osiek is their mutual "concern about the interrelationship between faith and works."[95] This concern may in fact be a natural result of their commitment to care for the poor, yet even if this is the case, that one would follow the other so closely (Hermas offers the two themes in *Vis* III.9 and III.6, respectively)in each text is likely more than coincidental. An incidental similarity between *James* 4:5 and *Mandate* III.1 is also noted. Osiek concludes these connections "are insufficient to conclude literary dependence. Both writings reflect the common world of Hellenistic Jewish moral instruction."[96] While literary dependence cannot be concluded, appealing to a general moral and/or philosophical mindset as the basis for such specific intersections seems insufficient. Many texts were written in the framework of Hellenistic Jewish moral instruction, yet the similarities between *James* and the work of Hermas are significant enough to show closeness in thought which goes beyond that general

---

[93] Ibid.

[94] Ibid.

[95] Ibid.

[96] Ibid.

framework. Some specific tradition or teaching, or a collection thereof, was likely in the minds of both James and Hermas when incorporating these concepts into their texts.

Osiek also notes a parallel between *Man.* II.4-6 and *Didache* 1.5. There, she states, "the sequence of three connections, at a few points with identical language, is notable."[97] The sequences in question are similar in structure and content, both exhorting the reader/hearer toward generosity to the poor. Both instruct their audience to give to all who ask, basing this instruction on the view that it is God who desires for such giving to take place. Each also absolves the giver of any misuse of the gift, declaring that he or she is innocent (ἀυω₁ος).[98] Noting the "considerable verbal variance," Osiek determines that "the best conclusion to draw is that there is a common written, or perhaps even oral, source behind the appearance of this one cluster of ideas in the two teachings."[99]

Stewart-Sykes' contribution to the discussion is noteworthy in that he is the only author referenced who sees a direct verbal connection to the Old Testament. *Mandate* VII.1-4 is, in his estimation, "a homily of the proemic type, a homily which begins with a scriptural citation impl(ying) that it is suited for homiletic use."[100] The scriptural citation in question, "Φοβητητι τόν κύριον και φύλασσε τάσ έντολάσ αύτου," is a quotation of *Ecclesiastes* 12:3 in VII.1, and its language is repeated throughout VII.2-4.

Stewart-Sykes further suggests that certain textual clues in the *Visions* give evidence that they are homilies.

> "Hermas, in describing his visions, three times addresses to himself to ἀδελφοί (*Vis.* 2.4, 3.1.1, 4.1.1), and at *Vis* 3.3.1 he tells the ancient lady that he intends to announce these visions to the brethren, in order that they may rejoice the more and know the Lord. These aims are surely homiletic aims."[101]

---

[97] Ibid. 27

[98] Ibid.

[99] Ibid.

[100] 1998. Hermas the Prophet and Hippolytus the Preacher. In *Preacher and Audience*, The Netherlands: Koninklijke Brill NV. 41

[101] Ibid. 42

He does not propose any Scripture or tradition upon which these homilies may have been based, and in fact appears unconcerned with whether such a relationship exists. This, however, conflicts with his later statement that the forms of homily he examined all had a "deep dependence on the scriptural text,"[102] and suggests a general orality, rather than an oral presentation which is specifically homiletic in nature.

Finally, Aune proposes that *Vision* II offers two conditional threats and promises, in which "we have a relatively clear allusion to the kind of tradition found in Mark 8:38 (and parallels) and Luke 12:9 (and parallel)." [103] While he does not advocate a specific literary relationship, he too affirms the likelihood of Hermas relying on traditions which were also used by the Synoptic authors.

IV. Missing References

The above sections present a strong case for some aspects of the *Shepherd* containing portions which are based on texts and traditions which would have had religious significance for Hermas' community. They show connections from all three sections of the *Shepherd* to texts in the Old and New Testaments, as well as at least one non-canonical tradition. However, even if we were to accept all of the above references as evidence of textual or traditional relationships, it would still leave a significant amount of the text without any basis in existing traditions. This is certainly an issue which needs to be addressed, but it does on its own discredit the theory. There are two possible explanations for this lack of reference, and each likely plays a part.

When dealing with references by one antique document to others, we are always limited by the fact that many potential sources are not presently extant for verification. The only text which Hermas acknowledges a reference to is *The Book of Eldad and Modat*,[104] which is one such example of a non-extant text. This problem is compounded when dealing with oral traditions, which may have never been committed to writing elsewhere. They may have been

---

[102] 2001.*Prophecy to Preaching*. 27

[103] 1983. *Prophecy in Early Christianity and the Ancient Mediterranean World*. Grand Rapids: William B. Eerdmans Publishing Company. 304

[104] *Vision* II.3.4

fallen out of vogue and not been considered important enough to take up space on a papyrus, or those carrying on the tradition might have seen Hermas' inclusion thereof as sufficient preservation in its own right. We cannot therefore know with any degree of certainty how much of the *Shepherd* is based in non-extant texts and traditions. They may provide the basis for the entire book, or they may play a relatively small part.

If there are portions of the text not based (at least partially) on prior texts and traditions, the reasoning of Stewart-Sykes may offer some insight as to why.

> "Exegesis moved to the centre of prophetic activity only when a working canon had been established; conversely, the movement towards an authoritative text helped to endanger the prophetic phenomenon. In the case of Hermas, there are occasional references to scripture, but the authority of scripture is on a par with the authority of the prophet."[105]

While I hope that the preceding arguments have demonstrated that Hermas' references to Scripture were more than occasional, this picture of dual sources of authority helps us to see why he may have been comfortable speaking extemporaneously on some matters, while appealing to sacred sources on others. Hermas was writing in a period of transition. There were no doubt certain beliefs of which his community would have rejected any contradictions or alterations, and he would therefore have had to insure compliance with existing tradition. However, there would also have been many questions whose answers were not pre-determined, and Hermas' role as a congregational prophet-in-residence would have given him the authority to draw his own conclusions on those matters.

The above evidence offers a strong basis for concluding that the *Shepherd* was originally a collection of homilies and prophetic oracles. Hermas' inclusion of the two in the same document, without commentary as to which is which, indicates that Hermas and his community had not yet developed a view of inspiration or authority which separated one from the other. In the following chapter, we will see how this blurring of the lines between prophecy and homily, along with Hermas' own theological agenda, creates a distinct homiletical style.

---

[105] 1998. Hermas the Prophet 41-42

4 the Homiletical Model(s) of the *Shepherd*

The homilies of Hermas are at the same time unique and yet unoriginal. A survey of Christian homileticians from the first century until the present day does not appear to yield a preacher whose methods are quite like Hermas'.[106] However, stepping outside of Christian tradition and looking toward the broader world of orality, his approach clearly has precedent. In the preceding chapter, the homiletical nature of the *Shepherd* was established by demonstrating how Hermas' writing makes use of formulae and themes found in traditions which his community found useful for instruction in faith. We will now take a closer look at the oral methods he used to convert scriptural tradition to original content.

I. Methods of Oral Poets

Casey Wayne Davis, building on the work of Albert Lord, establishes nine conclusions regarding how oral poets made use of formulas and themes.[107] Three of these conclusions are of particular interest when discussing Hermas' methodology. First, "With respect to themes, 'In a traditional poem... there is a pull in

---

[106] See Stewart-Sykes, Allistair, *Prophecy to Preaching* for an example of such a survey.

[107] *Oral Biblical Criticism*, 13-14

two directions: one is toward the song being sung and the other is toward previous uses of the same theme'. This can result in inconsistencies where two themes are brought together without meshing the facts of the two situations."[108]

The *Shepherd* is apparently not a work which is overly concerned with intrinsic contradictions. Hermas seems content to leave inconsistencies side by side, without commentary or explanation as to how both themes can be accurate when they appear to be in tension, or even outright disagreement. This is made clear from the very beginning of the text. Hermas' former mistress appears to him to tell him that she has been called upon to accuse him of sin.[109] Immediately after this, Hermas asks her if she is, in fact, accusing him, and she informs him that she is not.[110] The remainder of her message is a warning, and her character's literary function is not to serve as an accuser, but to prepare Hermas for the visions which are to come. Her self-stated purpose for appearing to him in verse five stands in direct contradiction to her statements in verse six and following, yet Hermas does not bother to explain or justify that contradiction.

Second, Davis establishes that "Singers may vary their telling of a story by the use of elaboration or simplification, expansion of ornamentation, changes of order in the sequence, addition of material not in a given text but found in the texts of singers from other districts, omission of material and 'substitution of one theme for another, in a story held together by inner tension.'"[111]

This can be demonstrated by examining any of the portions of the *Shepherd* which I have previously established as being based upon extant tradition. Hermas rearranges plot lines, combines themes from multiple stories, and elaborates upon the stories which he preserves.

---

[108] Ibid. 13

[109] *Vision* I.5

[110] Ibid. I.6

[111] *Oral Biblical Criticism*, 13

Third, "An oral poem made literate will tend to be longer and more episodic than its source."[112] This is one area where it is clear that the orality of the *Shepherd* is residual, not primary. If we read Jesus' parables in Mark as a more or less accurate preservation of their original form (insofar as it pertains to length), a significant difference in length becomes clear between them (the source), and the *Shepherd* (the poem).

It is through these three particular methods of adaptation that the style of Hermas emerges. Beginning with existing stories, Hermas expands upon them, introduces original content, combines (sometimes-contradicting) themes, and ultimately develops a finished product which communicates his intended message while preserving the messages of the source stories. The following sections will show how this method is applied to several extant traditions from which Hermas draws.

I. 1 Thessalonians 5:13 and *Vision* III

The language of *1 Thessalonians 5:13*[113] is woven into Hermas' third *Vision* three times, creating a recurring refrain which encourages the members of his community to be at peace with one another. This refrain underscores the larger theme being used in the vision of Christian community as tower. Blocks which are said to represent those who hurt the peace of the community are removed from the structure of the tower, and replaced by blocks representing more peaceful individuals.

The new story Hermas is telling demonstrates a pull to uses of the same theme in previous stories. Paul's use of the call to peace is as a self-contained statement, and its occurrence in *Vision* III.9.2 reflects this usage. The primary (possibly only) theme in III.9 is that of communal peace, making any elaboration subject to verse 2. However, Hermas also uses the statement to call other themes to mind. In section 6, for instance, the themes of communal peace and community as tower are woven together in such a way that a third theme is implied, without being explicitly stated. The non-peaceful

---

[112] Ibid. 14

[113] Any references to Scripture in this chapter assume the possibility that these passages are the preservation of oral traditions upon which Hermas also depended.

blocks are cracked and worn, such that if they were to remain in the structure, its integrity would be compromised. Non-peaceful members of a community create these cracks by causing division among the community members. So, without using the terminology, Hermas has reminded his community of Jesus' assertion in Mark 3:25 that a divided house cannot stand. Finally, in section 12, Hermas makes the receipt of further visions contingent upon communal peace. Several parts of the Jesus tradition indicate that God's knowledge is given to the peaceful.[114] Through expertly combining two themes, Hermas is able to communicate each one more effectively, while also connecting them to other themes which carry the message of the benefits of peacefulness.

As far as Hermas' method for varying his telling of the story, it is evident (as demonstrated above) that the incorporation of materials found in other stories is a major component. However, elaboration also plays a significant role in this sequence, as it does in many of his adaptations. A single liturgical refrain in *1 Thessalonians* is transformed into three sections in *Vision* III (as well as an additional section in *Similitude* VIII). How much of this is expansion, as opposed to a "more episodic" textual presentation of an oral tradition is not readily evident, but the fact that it is utilized on four separate occasions is sufficient to conclude that it is, at least in part, an instance of elaborative techniques.

II. *Ephesians* 2:19-22 and *Vision* III *Similitude* IX

While *1 Thessalonians* is utilized in the third *Vision*, it is not the primary text upon which the overall homily is based. That role is most likely filled by *Ephesians* 2:19-22. *Vision* III is one of two homilies which make extensive use of the building metaphor utilized by Paul in his letter to the Ephesians,[115] with *Similitude* IX serving as the second. In some ways, these homilies carry the underpinnings of

---

[114] Luke 19, for instance, suggests that Jerusalem's lack of peace has led to certain things being hidden from them by God.

[115] There are, of course, other texts which analogize the Christian community to a building, but given the evidence in previous chapters which indicates a strong support for a literary relationship between *Ephesians* and the *Shepherd*, this is the most likely source.

a classic diatribe-style homily. They are based on a relatively small segment of sacred tradition, follow a process of inductive reasoning, and are heavily analytic in nature. Yet the narrative form these sermons take goes a long way in masking the diatribe, and transforming it into something new and different.

Neither homily begins by stating that the Church is a building. Rather, they begin with an image of the building process, followed by an affirmation that these processes, as well as the buildings themselves, are representative of the church. In each instance, this affirmation segues into a description of the various elements of the building and the process, and which aspects of the Christian community they are meant to represent. By converting the opening statement and analytical explanation into a narrative, and submerging the didactic elements in that story, Hermas is able to transform the traditional diatribe into a story which is more appropriate for his audience. Then, by incorporating certain liturgical refrains (such as *1 Thessalonians* 5:13), he insures that the audience will recall the information presented.

The pull to previous telling is most evident in *Similitude* IX. Hermas introduces a Christ character in the form of a nobleman who is portrayed as the owner of the tower being built. That he is meant to be Christ cannot be disputed, as he is later described by the Shepherd as ὁ υἱος τοῦ θεοῦ. Even so, when Hermas asks the Shepherd what is represented by the rock upon which the tower is built, he is told that this is also ὁ υἱος τοῦ θεοῦ, perhaps because the passage in Ephesians labels the corner stone as Jesus Christ. The gate of the tower is also identified as ὁ υἱος τοῦ θεοῦ, with the explanation that God's Son is the only gate by which people can enter the Christian community. These three instances of ὁ υἱος τοῦ θεοῦ in such close proximity to one another represent a desire to remain true to the original story, to communicate Hermas' intended message, and possibly to give a nod to another tradition, such as that in *John* 10:9, with which his community was familiar.

Once again, elaboration plays a significant role in the process. *Vision* III expands on *Ephesians* 2, and *Similitude* IX expands further on *Vision* III. A passage of about two lines is ultimately expanded into thirty-three sections of detail and explanation, with multiple themes inserted to fill out the body of the narrative. Every aspect of the building, from the materials and their sources, to the building process, to the inspection and correction of errors, to the completion of the project and cleaning up of the work site are discussed in detail, and each aspect has its own allegorical meaning. The finished homily explores every possible facet of the original passage, even delving into multiple components of the building which were in all likelihood not in the mind of the original author.

III. The *Kenosis Hymn* and *Similitude* V

The homily which most fully reflects Hermas' methodological approach to his homilies is found in *Similitude* V. Its correlation to the *Kenosis Hymn* was demonstrated in Chapter 3, as was its utilization of the Jesus Parable tradition. It may be because Hermas chose a narrative, oral tradition for his base theme that his homiletic model is realized most fully in this particular sermon. The root theme of the *Kenosis Hymn* is combined with the broader Jesus Parable tradition, and influenced by theological presuppositions which contradict those held by the authors of the original text.

Hermas is pulled strongly by the previous telling of the *Kenosis Hymn*, making sure to correlate a portion of his vision to each line of the hymn, as illustrated in the following table:

Philippians 2:6-11	*Similitude* V
6	V.6.1
7	V.2.2
8	V.2.3-4
9	V.2.5-7
10-11	V.2.8-9

Table 4.1

The initial parable which the Shepherd tells Hermas casts Son of God in the role of a servant, causing it to correspond with the second line of the *Kenosis Hymn*. The remainder of the parable follows the pattern established by the hymn, resulting in a near- one to one correlation. However, the exclusion of the first line does not go unnoticed by Hermas. Some reading this similitude and its explanation are inclined to understand Hermas as an Adoptionist, and a straightforward reading of the parable certainly lends credence to such an understanding. Yet it is clear from *Similitude* V.6.1 that Hermas also saw the problem in the parable, and took steps to correct it. He has the Shepherd contradict the parable, asserting that the Son of God is *not* portrayed as a servant, but rather as a powerful being. This both diffuses the issue of Adoptionism, and brings the parable in line with the hymn by providing a statement which corresponds to the initially-excluded first line. That Hermas was willing to insert a contradicting statement several paragraphs into a detailed explanation in order to bring the parable into harmony with the hymn (and out of harmony within itself) shows how strong the pull was to the original telling.

That *Similitude* V is "longer and more episodic than its source,"[116] is without question. The *Kenosis Hymn* is a scant 7 lines of text. Each verse in *Similitude* V is longer than its corresponding verse in the hymn, such that the parable alone is 56 lines, and it is accompanied by an additional five sections of explanation, each of which is dozens of lines long. Even if one were to take into account the other source materials Hermas may have borrowed from the Jesus Parable Tradition, the resulting *Similitude* is still several times the length of the sum of the lengths of the sources.

As for modification, *Similitude* V is variegated and nuanced in its approach. While elaboration undoubtedly takes center stage in this homily, just as it does in the others, the other aspects of alteration are used more thoroughly than in his other homilies. The incorporation of the parabolic traditions is extensive; while other homilies merely alluded to additional traditions, or included one or two familiar lines, the story in the *Similitude* artfully combines several parables[117] into one new, distinct parable, which conveys the narrative of the base text. Hermas also decides to make a slight rearrangement of the themes found in the source, relocating the first theme to a later point (as illustrated above).

The resulting homily is a detailed exposition of its source. Yet it is even more than that. It is a narrative which the audience can easily remember. It is a series of familiar and compelling images. And above all, it is the most complete model we have of the homiletical method which made the *Shepherd* a valued book which would be preserved against the test of time.

---

[116] Davis, Casey Wayne. *Oral Biblical Criticism* 14

[117] Four, if the delineation in Chapter 3 is correct.

IV. Defining Hermas' Model

The approach Hermas uses is both sophisticated and simple. While an exact routine or step-by-step method cannot be identified, a general understanding of the components of his writing process can be cleaned from the homilies examined above. He identifies his primary text, and goes about exegesis in much the same way that a technical preacher might. The text, its main themes, subordinate themes, context within the larger text (if any), and context within society are taken into account. Hermas also identifies other sacred texts and traditions which emphasize the themes of the primary text. This utilization of supporting texts is again an approach which is a standard aspect of analytical and expository sermon writing. It is what Hermas does once he has compiled this information which makes his method so distinct.

Having identified the theological, ethical, or practical teachings which he wishes to communicate, Hermas then submerges them within a narrative structure. The premise for the narrative is a simple image or series of images with which Hermas' audience would have been readily familiar. The primary didactic measure is the dialog of the characters in the narrative, which extracts the intended instructions from the image by use of leading questions and other conversational cues. When the sermon is complete, the audience has learned what Hermas intended, and has learned it in such a way that they will be able to recall it in the future. A familiar image has been imbued with meaning, and the important aspects of that image have been highlighted and explained within the course of the narrative. By using this method, Hermas is assured that the hearers of his sermons will be likely to remember both the content and the message of those sermons.

V. Conclusion

Stories (and by extension, storytellers) have long been the primary means for captivating an audience and sharing one's ideas. With the rise of literacy in the Western world, the stories people told were more and more preserved by text, and the written word became the most popular medium for the dissemination of ideas. This did not deter storytellers from having significant influence; indeed, the most well-known texts from almost any time period tend to be narratives and works of fiction. However, the utilization of text as a tool for encoding information also led to a rise in more technical approaches to knowledge, particularly in post-enlightenment civilizations. Analytical texts were produced, lists were made, and "objectivity" became increasingly important. However, recent decades have shown a new trend rising. The primary medium of storytelling in our culture has become that of film, and with the rising popularity of film has come a return to experiential learning and a dependence upon imagery. Even films which are adapted from books often find broader audiences than those texts upon which they are based. Whether this is a result of the so-called "Postmodern turn," or simply a cultural shift resulting from the rise of a new medium is unimportant. What is important is that the contemporary Western culture has once again become reliant upon narrative and image, perhaps more so than at any time since the rise of ubiquitous literacy.[118]

With this newfound dependence upon imagery comes a need for contemporary homileticians to restyle their approaches to preaching. The analytical, technically proficient homily which was so effective in a text-based culture will not be the most efficient means of communication in a culture built on imagery. Contemporary homileticians can utilize the method which I have outlined above, thereby catering to their image-dependent audiences.[119] In seeking a new approach to homiletics, I propose that the one established by Hermas, and defined in the preceding chapters, could be sufficient in providing a working model.

---

[118] Many texts have been dedicated to this particular shift in communication media. See for instance Mitchell Stephens' *The Rise of the Image, the Fall of the Word.* 1998, Oxford University Press.

[119] I have provided one such utilization in the appendix which follows this chapter.

Appendix

The following is the second chapter of a Bible study curriculum entitled "In the Garden of Joy," which I wrote using the model described in Chapter 4 of this text. Its root text is Philippians 1:12-14.

      I woke up the next morning, realizing that the gardener had not told me what time I was to meet him, but I drove to the address scrawled on the sheet of paper, expecting to arrive his house shortly after breakfast. Needless to say, I was a bit taken aback to discover that the address I had been given was not to a house, but to a garden. I looked at the paper again, and back at the garden; yes, this was definitely 122 Rome Lane. A sign over the gate read "St. Paul Community Memorial Garden." As I got out of my car, it occurred to me that I really should not have been all that surprised at the choice of location- this was probably one of the places where the gardener worked.

      Before I could reflect any further, I heard a now-familiar voice call out "Hail, Phil." There he stood at the gate, dressed just as he had been the day before, waving a trowel at me in greeting. "Welcome to St. Paul's, Phil. Come with me, I have much to show you."

We began our walk in silence, and I took the opportunity to survey the garden. It was a sight to behold! Everywhere I looked, the place was in full bloom. Flowers opened gaily on every stem, and every tree and shrub looked green and full. Some plots eschewed flowering plants in favor of small vegetable gardens, and it was obvious their owners could look forward to a bountiful harvest. There didn't appear to be a weed in the place, or if there was, even it was a beautiful sight to behold. I could have spent the whole day admiring the work of those tending their plots, but my own gardener"s voice interrupted my admiration.

"Do you know the story of St. Paul"s, Phil?"

"No, I didn't even know this place was here until just now," something I was quickly beginning to regret.

"You are not alone. This garden is one of the best kept secrets in town, and even most of those who hold plots here do not know how it began. Years ago, this area was unsettled terrain. The road had not been built, the land had not been leveled, and this spot was just a clearing in an otherwise unremarkable forest. The man who owned this land happened upon the clearing on day, and decided that it would be a good place to have a garden. The clearing was nearly a mile from his house, through brush and brambles and mud, yet he came every day to tend the land. He found that the soil here was quite fertile, and soon his little plot was producing all manner of fruits and vegetables, larger and riper than any he had ever seen. The man came faithfully to his garden every day for many years, but he grew old and weak, and in time he was no longer able to make the journey to the clearing or care for the plants himself. His neighbors, who had always enjoyed the fruits of his labor, saw this, and began to make the journey to the clearing in his stead. First they went one at a time, then they traveled in twos and threes, and in time they found that they all loved the place as much as he had, and each one wanted to go to the garden every day.

"Their constant traffic wore down a path to the clearing, and thanks to their labor, the garden was even more fruitful than it had been when the man cared for it himself. In his gratitude, he arranged for his neighbors to receive his land when he died. They turned the path into a road, and built houses on either side, each claiming a small piece of the inheritance, but the garden they made a public place, and a memorial in honor of the man who began it."

Hear Then, the Parable

I looked around the garden with fresh eyes, amazed that all of this- the flowers, the trees, the vegetables, the road, even the houses!- were the result of one man's hard work. "Wow," was all I could say.

"Do you understand why I have brought you here and told you this, Phil?" His question surprised me. "I... I thought you were just telling me about the garden. Was that a true story, or another one of your 'parables'?"

"It was both. Every word I spoke was true, but this story is the parable of the first virtue."

"Then I'm lost. It's a beautiful story, but I don't know what it's supposed to mean," I stared at my feet, wanting to hide my embarrassment.

"The man who found the clearing is every saint who has ever done the work of God, and the garden is that saint's work. Does this help you understand, or shall I explain further?"

I was sad to admit it, but too curious to let my shame stop me. "Tell me more," I whispered.

"Every person is like the old, weak man. Some become ill, some lose sight or speech, and some are even captured or imprisoned, but all eventually find some obstacle to doing the work of God. But even in that hindrance, the faithful trust that the Lord"s work will continue, and their lives demonstrate that trust. The man was faithful to his garden, and when he grew old, he was able to trust that his neighbors would carry on his work. So also you, when you find yourself hindered in doing the work you have been given, can trust that the Lord is even now prompting others to overcome the obstacles which you cannot. So the first virtue is this: Trust in the Lord."

"But I cannot see God, or know when these other people are being prompted to help me. How am I supposed to trust?"

"Neither could the old man see his garden, but the product of the neighbors' labor was undeniable. So also you will see the fruit of those who work on your behalf, if you will trust in the Lord."

I wanted to protest further, but I knew the gardener was right. Silently I asked God to help me to trust more.

Bibliography

1. The New Testament in the Apostolic Fathers. 1905.
2. Aune, David E. 1983. *Prophecy in Early Christianity and the Ancient Mediterranean World.* Vol. . Grand Rapids: William B. Eerdmans Publishing Company.
3. Bagnall, Roger S. 2009. *Early Christian Books in Egypt.* Princeton: Princeton University Press.
4. Davis, Casey Wayne. 1999. Oral Biblical Criticism. *Journal for the Study of the New Testament Supplement Series* 172.
5. Holmes, Michael W. 2007. *The Apostolic Fathers: Greek Texts and English Translations.* 3rd ed. Grand Rapids: Baker Academic.
6. Lord, Albert Bates. 1960. *The singer of tales, Harvard studies in comparative literature ; 24.* Cambridge: Harvard University Press.
7. McClure, John S. 1991. *The Four Codes of Preaching.* Minneapolis: Augsburg Fortress Press.
8. McDonald, James I. H. 1980. *Kerygma and Didache.* Edited by R. M. Wilson, *Society for New Testament Studies Monograph Series.* New York: Cambridge University Press.
9. Muddiman, John. 2005. The Church in Ephesians, 2 *Clement*, and the *Shepherd of Hermas.* In *Trajectories through the New Testament and Apostolic Fathers*, edited by A. F. Gregory and C. M. Tuckett. New York: Oxford University Press.
10. Ong, Walter. 1982. *Orality and Literacy: The Technologizing of the Word.* London: Methuen
11. Osiek, Carolyn. 1998. The Oral World of Early Christianity in Rome: The Case of Hermas. In *Judaism and Christianity in First-Century Rome*, edited by K. P. Donfried and P. Richardson. Grand Rapids: Wm. B Eerdmans Publishing Co.
12. -- 1999. *Shepherd of Hermas: A Commentary on the Shepherd of Hermas.* Edited by H. Koester, *Hermeneia.* Minneapolis: Augsburg Fortress Press.
13. Parry, Milman. 1930. Studies in the epic technique of oral verse-making. I. Homer and the Homeric Style. *Harvard Studies in Classical Philology* 41:73-147.

14. Stewart-Sykes, Alistair. 1998. Hermas the Prophet and Hippolytus the Preacher. In *Preacher and Audience*, edited by M. B. Cunningham and P. Allen. Leiden, The Netherlands: Koninklijke Brill NV.
15. -- 2001. *From Prophecy to Preaching.* Edited by J. Den Boeft, R. Van Den Broek, W. L. Petersen, D. T. Runia and J. C. M. Van Winden. Vol. LIX, *Supplements to Vigiliae Christianae*. Leiden, the Netherlands: Koninklijke Brill.
16. Stephens, Mitchell. 1998. *The Rise of the Image: The Fall of the Word*. New York: Oxford University Press

Printed in Great Britain
by Amazon